better together*

*This book is best read together, grownup and kid.

 akidsco.com

a
kids
book
about

a kids book about diversity

by Charnaie Gordon

A Kids Co.
Editor Denise Morales Soto
Designer Duke Stebbins
Creative Director Rick DeLucco
Studio Manager Kenya Feldes
Sales Director Melanie Wilkins
Head of Books Jennifer Goldstein
CEO and Founder Jelani Memory

DK
Editor Emma Roberts
Senior Production Editor Jennifer Murray
Senior Production Controller Louise Minihane
Senior Acquisitions Editor Katy Flint
Acquisitions Project Editor Sara Forster
Managing Art Editor Vicky Short
Publishing Director Mark Searle
DK would like to thank Patrice Lawrence

This American Edition, 2024
Published in the United States by DK Publishing
1745 Broadway, 20th Floor, New York, NY 10019

DK books are available at special discounts when purchased in bulk for
sales promotions, premiums, fund-raising, or educational use. For details, contact:
DK Publishing Special Markets, 1745 Broadway, 20th Floor, New York, NY 10019, or SpecialSales@dk.com

Printed and bound in China

www.dk.com

akidsco.com

To my husband, who has given me unconditional friendship and love for 20 years.

To my kids, Madison and Barrington: your growth provides a constant source of joy and pride.

To the reader: it is my hope that this book might help make the world a better place.

Intro
for grownups

Have you ever had a hard time fitting in? At school, with a new group of friends, or even in your own family? Or, maybe there was a time you had trouble accepting someone else? Every person can probably relate to feeling they aren't welcome at one time or another. That's where the power of stories can come into play.

I believe stories are the key to building greater empathy and creating shared understanding. Consider how different the world would look if we all accepted each other for who we are. To see others and allow them to just be. When you accept people, you make space for them to feel the way they want to feel, to be different and think differently from you—that's what diversity is.

This book is designed to help kids and grownups learn to appreciate and accept others. To teach us that it's OK to notice differences, but more importantly, that differences are a really good thing to celebrate.

Enjoy!

Have you ever...

thought about the superheroes in movies?

Or the characters in your favorite story?

Or in the cartoons you like?

How many of them...

look like you?

have families like yours?

dress like you?

have the same
skin color as you?

Think about this before you turn the page.

Now, let me introduce myself.

My name is Charnaie, and I'd like to share what I know about **diversity** with you.

"What's that?"

you may be wondering,

**"and what does
it have to do with
superheroes?"**

Diversity means *difference.*

People are the same in some ways, but different in others.

We all have different *hair types, eye color,* and *skin tones.*

Some people wear *glasses* or *contact lenses,* but *others don't.*

There are people who are *really tall* and there are people who are *really short.*

Diversity is everything that makes you, **you!**

**Your age,
skin color,
gender identity,
religion or beliefs,
heritage,
ethnicity,
sexuality,
disability,
socioeconomic status,*
political views or beliefs,
and so much more!**

*Socioeconomic status means how you are identified in society, according to things like how much schooling you have, how much money you make, and what your job is.

When we include and accept people from every background and perspective,
we embrace diversity and celebrate those differences that make us special.

Now, about those characters and superheroes you thought about before—chances are most of them are:

white, nondisabled, cisgender,* males.

*cisgender: when a person's gender identity matches the sex they were assigned at birth.

There's nothing wrong with being white, or nondisabled, or cisgender, or male!

Everyone has their own unique perspective that they bring into the mix.

But think about how exciting it might be to know there's a superhero like you!

Don't you think everyone should have that?

We live in a big,
beautiful, and diverse world!

It's *full* of different...

people
perspectives
experiences
stories
ideas
colors
music
memories
dance moves
traditions
food
beliefs
holidays

When we don't include people who are different from us, we miss out on so many wonderful things.

That's why diversity is important.

When we embrace each other's diversity...

Everyone can experience themselves reflected in the world around them.

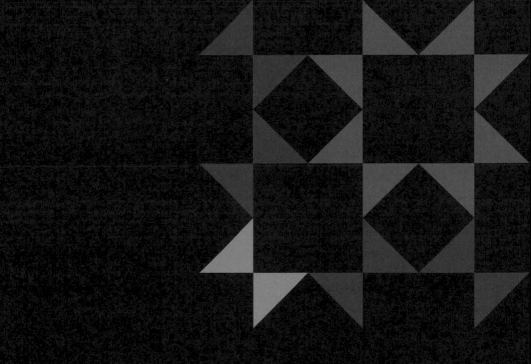

People can experience others being the hero of a story.

Negative stereotypes get smashed, which leads to more acceptance and everyone being nicer to one another.

And we can learn so much about other people.

Other people's lives and experiences matter— and so do yours!

When we embrace diversity, we give others the freedom to be themselves.

And when we see others free to be themselves, we can feel safe to be ourselves too.

When I was a kid,

there weren't a lot of people who looked like me in cartoons, books, or movies.

This made me feel like my life was less important than the lives of other people......

....Then one day,

I turned on the TV and finally saw someone who looked like me who wasn't an athlete, rapper, or singer.

It was Oprah!

She instantly became my role model.

I wanted to be just like her.

She made me feel seen, understood, and less alone.

Today, things are
a lot different.

There is more diversity
in books, TV, movies,
and the people who are
in charge—but we still
have a long way to go.

Can you think of a main character in a TV show who is deaf?

Can you think of a leader who is Indigenous?

Can you think of a scientist who isn't a man?

Did you think of anyone?
How long did it take you?
Did you have to look it up?

Now, take a step back and take a good look at the diversity in *your* life.

Do you see it in your neighborhood?

How about your school?

Friend group?

Community?

We can do better.

We have to do better.

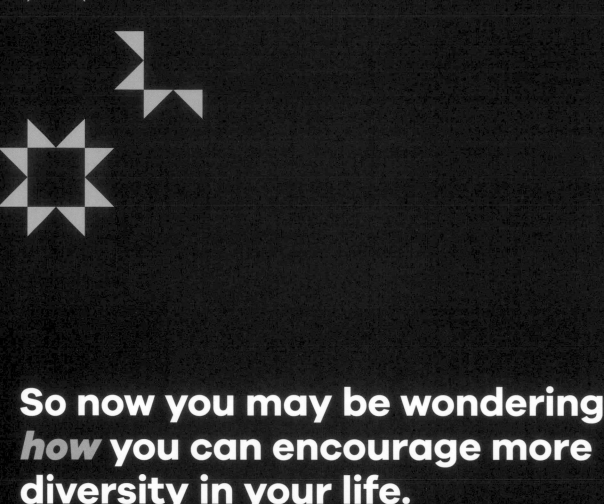

So now you may be wondering *how* you can encourage more diversity in your life.

There are a lot of things you can do!

Embrace who you are.

Don't be afraid of being different.

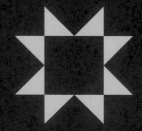

Be open to learning about other people and their lives.

Everyone has something unique to share.

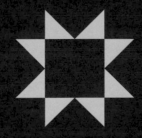

Look for books with characters who are different from you.*

*If you don't find yourself in books, write your own!

Talk to kids who have different beliefs from you.

What traditions do they have?

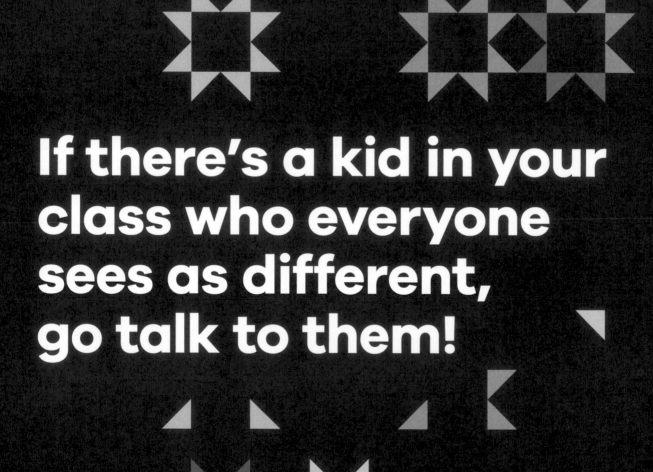

If there's a kid in your class who everyone sees as different, go talk to them!

Play games that you've never heard of before.

They might be fun!

Try food that you've never tasted before and find the place where it's from on a map!

Learn other ways to communicate with people.

Try a new language, like Spanish or a signed language!

Talk to a grownup about the many types of diversity.

Be curious,
ask questions,
and LISTEN.

DIVERSITY IS NORMAL.

Diversity is like a kaleidoscope, filled with lots of colors, shapes, and textures.

If we're all willing to peek inside, we'll open our minds to a beautiful world filled with more kindness, empathy, love, and respect.

So if you notice you are resisting diversity—→

embrace it
instead!

Let's smash hate, prejudice, racism, and discrimination.

And celebrate what makes each person unique.

Outro
for grownups

Now that you know what diversity is and different ways you can help your kid add more diversity to their life, what's the next step? Books can serve as a great starting point to having big conversations, but what matters most is that you take action and apply the information you've learned to your everyday life.

Books can also be powerful tools, but they aren't fast solutions. I can tell you from experience that, as with many things, you will get back what you put in. Changing culture and mindsets is hard work, but with consistent, focused attention coupled with action, it is possible.

If we truly want to live in a more equitable world, it should be the responsibility of us all to create an environment that's free from prejudice and discrimination. Embracing diversity is the first step. Let's normalize creating a rich and diverse world together for our children and our future.

Who is with me?

About The Author

Charnaie Gordon (she/her) is an African American wife, mom, author, entrepreneur, and lifelong learner. She lives in Connecticut with her husband and 2 kids. Charnaie enjoys providing strategies for diversifying your bookshelves and empowering families to instill a love of reading and curiosity in their kids. She wrote *A Kids Book About Diversity* to help kids and families understand what diversity is and how to actively embrace it in every aspect of their lives.

Charnaie's passion for diversity and inclusion is driven by a desire for everyone to have their own voice, whether it be through books, television, or other media. She believes it's important that people of all ethnic backgrounds can see themselves represented and included.

 @hereweeread   @hereweeread   @hereweeread

Made to empower.

a kids book about **racism**
by Jelani Memory

a kids book about ANXIETY
by Ross Szabo

a kids book about DISABILITY
by Kristine Napper
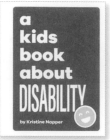

a kids book about IMAGINATION
by LEVAR BURTON

a kids book about *belonging*
by Kevin Carroll

a kids book about **failyure**
by Dr. Laymon Hicks

a kids book about GRATITUDE
by Ben Kenyon

a kids book about LIFE ONLINE
by Dave S. Anderson & Blake Fleischacker

a kids book about *body image*
by Rebecca Alexander

a kids book about IMMIGRATION
by MJ Calderon

a kids book about EMPATHY
by Daron K. Roberts

a kids book about GENDER
by Dale Mueller

a kids book about Love
by ZIGGY MARLEY
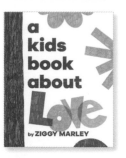

a kids book about EQUALITY
by BILLIE JEAN KING

a kids book about MONEY
by Adam Stramwasser

a kids book about **FEMINISM**
by Emma Mcilroy

a kids book about *adventure*
by Dr. Ben Tertin

a kids book about CLIMATE CHANGE
by Zanagee Artis & Olivia Greenspan

a kids book about CONFIDENCE
by Joy Cho

a kids book about BEING NONBINARY
by Hunter Chinn-Raicht